Death without Dying

Robin S. Anthony

authorHOUSE®

AuthorHouse™
1663 Liberty Drive
Bloomington, IN 47403
www.authorhouse.com
Phone: 1 (800) 839-8640

Published by AuthorHouse 12/06/2016

ISBN: 978-1-5246-4894-7 (sc)
ISBN: 978-1-5246-4893-0 (e)

Chapters

Dear Mom,

I write this letter to you to give me closure. I found out a few weeks ago that you passed away. I guess I don't feel sorrow or grief! I just feel numb. Pierre and Dawn never contacted me, I found out through a nurse that worked at the Coyne House.

You never called me to see if I was doing all right. You knew Robert's house was a mess and he is an alcoholic. Let me just give you a run down of how life has been for me the last six years.

I lost EVERYTHING! I have no family. I have friends but no one can help me through the terrible journey I have to take.

- I lost all my money that I saved. I hired a dumpster for $395.00 to clean the house and Robert put everything back within hours of my hiring the dumpster.
- I had to contend with Robert's friends stealing my things and being a threat to my safety.
- Robert was drunk most of the time and he broke most of my things.
- I had to walk every place a lot of the times in all kinds of weather.
- Robert forced me to buy a car that was a lemon for $2,500 and I had to have it towed.
- I lost my beloved Yorkshire terrier Susie Q on August 5, 2008 because Robert will not fix the door. She had the value of $900.00 but the point is I miss her and I will never get her back.
- The furnace is unsafe and I am always afraid of fire.
- The ceiling leaks every time it rains in the bathroom and the kitchen.
- The toilet backed up on the clothes that I am forced to keep in the kitchen and ruined them.
- Robert won't give me a bedroom and the clutter is deplorable.
- Valerie and Lynn do not want to bother with me because of the way I live.
- I had a nervous break down in 2008 and now can only work at Trudy's between 3 and 12 hours a week.

- Robert expects me to pay for everything and I had to give him $2,500 for his transmission on top of everything else I lost.
- I can't take a bath in the tub because the tub is filthy.
- I can't watch TV because there is no signal.
- I am trapped in his filthy house from morning to night because I don't have a car.
- He once hit me in an argument that we had.
- The yard is filthy and the fences are broken and I have to worry about the dogs when they are outside.
- I have met undesirable people in my life that took advantage of me because of my dire situation.
- I tried to rent a room and the couple were drug addicts and I never got my security deposit back.

Well my life is ruined. I have been to the hospital countless times for stress related illness. I lost $630.00 to hire a handwriting expert and $1,000.00 for the defense lawyer to defend me. The probation officer put a warrant on my license and I had to return to court to drop the charges that Pierre put against me.

You did NOTHING TO PROTECT ME OR THE DOGS.

You signed the second deed leaving the house to Pierre and Dawn when I had no place to live.

I WILL NEVER FORGIVE YOU FOR THAT!

I used to believe in God and an afterlife. I am not sure there is a God or a place called heaven. If there is a heaven I hope you are not there.

I hope I do not encounter you in another life!!!

I can't undo the damage you allowed to enter my life. My life is forever tarnished and I know I will never truly be happy again.

I only look for peace of mind now in the future if I even have a future.

If there is a God he may be the one to forgive you because I never will.

Robin

P.S. I rescued another little dog named Hot Pocket for $1,000.00 and I lost her to a dental disease.

Dec 5, 2014

This book is dedicated to Susie Q, Lucy, Jon Pierre, Hot Pocket, Stevie Nicks, Fatima, Noelle, and Nicky.

To those of you running at Rainbow Bridge, I love and miss you and long to join you one day running amidst the butterflies.

To Fatima, Noelle, and Nicky, I am grateful for each day that you shower me with your wet kisses and let me pet your silky fur. I love you.

To my birds, Michael, Selena and Richard Jr., you make me laugh with your silly antics and tricks Even though I am constantly cleaning your cages I cherish you dearly.

To Humphrey, I love you and appreciate seeing you lay under your heat lamp in the kitchen.

To my Higher Power whom I choose to call God – Thank you for giving me the strength to carry on. You don't make my journey easy but it is NEVER BORING and you make me a stronger person each day.

To my precious friends Pam, Kelley, and Diane, thank you for your love, support and kindness.

Last not least by any means;

To Robert – I care for you deeply and want the best for you even though we have had our ups and downs. We walked the journey of laughter and tears, anger, peace, and sharing in the last ten years.

To my readers…

Please know that this story is a personal one. The accounts I have written are true and I have recorded them accurately to the best of my abilities.

I only pray that there will be someone or many who read this and know there is HOPE, and HELP. You are not alone and you can make it through the storm and manage to find the light of day. NEVER GIVE UP TRYING! ALWAYS LOVE and FORGIVE YOURSELF! You are lovable and capable and worthy of being happy and loved.

Life is a highway. Ride the road and enjoy the journey.

Robin

January 8, 2016

Foreword

On March 16, 2006 Pierre, Dawn and Anna put me out of the house that I lived in all my life.

My Childhood Home

They seized most of my belongings. Pierre forged Jo Ann's name on the deed of the house so he could give the house to his daughter Anna where she is living now. He did this with the help of the lawyer Fred. He did this while Jo Ann was in the hospital suffering from a stroke.

Pierre coerced her to sign a second deed giving him the rights to the childhood home property. Anna Marie should not be a doctor who works with people who have emotional problems. She treated me very poorly and unprofessionally. I did prove that Pierre committed forgery and as soon as I proved it he made sure Jo Ann signed another deed.

He did not notify me of my mother's death and posted her obituary on my YouTube page. On October 27, 2015 I have a saved message from Dawn on my smartphone.

- We are trying to contact you regarding an account your mother left. Contact Pierre or Dawn.
- Robin why did you wait so long? You need money to remodel your inn. Is there not another home that could use a forgery to obtain your money? Good luck, Dawn. We have not owned the inn for over five years. If you want to receive money left send me your address so the bank can contact you.

I gave Pierre and Dawn the address of a friend. I am not living at that address. THERE IS NO MONEY. THEY ARE JUST UP TO NO GOOD!

My conscience is clear. I am a TRUE SURVIVOR. I have written a true account of all the events that have happened to me.

Robin S Anthony

In the year 2016 I am moving forward with a positive attitude. Life has ups and downs but I can conquer any obstacle that comes into my path. Pierre, Dawn and Anna thought I would crumble and die when they put me out of the house. NOT so! There is life beyond my childhood home. I have a lot of accomplishments. I am a certified peer specialist, an author, singer, actress. I have turned lemons into lemonade. Not to mention that on November 15, 2015 I had a three and a half pound tumor removed from my shoulder. I am doing FINE.

PIERRE AND DAWN HAVE NOT RUINED MY LIFE.

I am STRONG!

I am HONEST!

I am HARDWORKING!

I AM A TRUE FRIEND TO MY FRIENDS. AS THE SONG SAYS, "I AM WOMAN".

Note: as for Robert and I we are moving in different directions. We will always remain connected in this vast universe. Remember, life is short. FORGIVE, FORGET and LIVE ONE MOMENT AT A TIME. You may never get another, enjoy.

Robin

Chapter One

Darkness

It all started when I was five years old. I suffered from depression and anxiety. My father was very ill so that experience traumatized me. I knew I was different from my peers, never quite fitting in or feeling "good enough".

I escaped into a world of fantasy. I had a very vivid imagination. I conjured up fantasies where I was the "special character" in my play. I did splendid, heroic things. I had imaginary friends who were beautiful, smart, and creative. I preferred them to my real life family and the few friends that I had.

I was called "weird" by my family. My mother told me to act "normal". "What is normal?" Is normal to be rude and aggressive like my older brother, who was "deemed a genius" but had no soul or substance in his personality? Was normal my sister who had a creative side but was vulgar and mean-spirited? I guess my parents thought they were "normal" but in their eyes I was a "zero".

I began my fantasy life of wanting to be an actress when I grew up. I loved music, singing, listening to the radio. I pranced around in party dresses on a Saturday night dancing like the beautiful girls in the "Lawrence Welk show". I longed to look like them.

Most of my childhood was dark and bizarre, sadness, pain, obsession with God and death. I was afraid to die yet I was fascinated with the concept. I read books about death and watched movies about people dying all the time. I loved it. The sadness fit my severe mood swings and it gave me reason to cry. I cried all the time. I cried when I was happy, sad and in-between. I was a professional mourner.

I lied a lot too. I made up stories for attention. I wanted my parents to notice me, think I had something important to say. I wanted to be SOMEBODY. Most of the time they told me to "shut up" and "go do something useful".

Mental illness is a TABOO! My mother tells me to hide it; stop whining or no one will want me if I don't act "normal". There is that word "normal" again. I don't know what it means except she keeps telling me I'm not. I walk my dark journey for years.

I am sheltered by my parents but not cherished. I have fears, phobias, and terrible temper tantrums. I want my way all the time and if I don't get it I become a raging, spoiled brat. I say mean things to people when I am angry. I am angry a lot. I feel guilty too for my behavior.

I love and hate my mother. I am attached to her apron strings. I don't want to share her affections with my brother and sister. They hate and resent me. I love my father in a distant way. I believe he can't meet my needs as my mother can.

I am constantly afraid of losing my parents. If my mother dies my whole world will be over. I will want to die with her. Who will take care of me? I am terrified of being along. I do love my aunt who is like a second mother to me. However she can't take the place of my mother.

I hate school. I do not want to take the school bus. The other children bully me. I am afraid of missing the bus and not getting home. My father drives me to school and waits for me in the parking lot. He gets caught by the principal and is told that he can drop me off at school and pick me up when school is over. NO MORE WAITING IN THE PARKING LOT! I am devastated. My fears and insecurities rise to the surface. I can't concentrate on my schoolwork. I once tell a teacher that, "I want to kill myself." She calls my parents and they have a special meeting about me.

My parents, Aunt, and my teachers agree it is time to find me help. I go to special classes and a well known Hospital in Boston to see a therapist. I have a "lazy eye" and allergies, which add to my anxiety. I am scared of my doctors. I do not want to be away from my parents.

The doctors ask me why I am so sad all the time. I just say, "I don't know". My parents have to talk to therapists about how they feel about my behavior. They want to know if I can be "normal" again. I never do become "normal" as my parents had hoped.

Chapter Two

Falling into Frustration

As a teenager I thought about killing myself most of the time. I felt ugly, stupid, and awkward compared to all the kids in my class. I went through school in a fog. I could not wait for the first day of summer and I always dreaded the first day of fall. In junior high school, I started to take an interest in my classes; science fiction and writing short stories intrigued me. I picked up my grades. I started to make friends.

In 1976, my beloved Aunt died and I was devastated. I went on to high school with a heavy heart for the first two years. I did not care about my grades or classes. My depression became worse when I was sixteen. I was in therapy but I was anxious and angry. Isolation became a huge part of my world. I went through a period where I gave my brother and sister a "good piece of my mind". They don't bother with me today.

I looked older than my age and I had a shapely, sexy figure. I tried to entice men by the way I dressed and flaunted around. I would never go all the way with sex. I was just delighted in the idea they thought I was attractive. I became obsessed with my looks, hair, clothes, and weight. At one point in my life I suffered from an eating disorder.

In my junior year of high school I began to regain interest in my subjects again. I took Early Childhood classes and decided to graduate. I enjoyed my senior year. I went to the senior reception and had a graduation party. I wanted to take a break from school so I worked at a few part time jobs.

Chapter Three

Trying to be an Adult

I had trouble holding down jobs because of my anxiety and depression. Sometimes I could not complete the tasks that were given to me. I was often left feeling useless. If I lost a job my mother would try to console me. She said I would find another job soon. My Aunt Teresa worked at an Engineering Firm in Boston. There were options and I went to work to be a filing clerk. I could not get the hang of it. The company did not let me go. They sent me to a special training program with people that had all types of disabilities. I was there to find out which tasks I could succeed at.

The training was for one week. I took many IQ tests, answered pretend phones, and took down messages. They picked and probed my brain. I talked to behavior therapists. At one point in my childhood they thought I had dyslexia. A doctor ruled that out because I was an excellent reader. Finally they decided that I was to be a mail clerk after my training ended. I went back to the Engineering Firm and delivered mail to four hundred engineers on the 14th floor. I memorized their names on my side of the building. I helped my co-worker with her share of the work as well. I liked my job as a mail clerk but I wanted more. I took night classes in Early Childhood Education and worked during the day. I felt restless and unsettled. I was not content. I experienced time of elation when I was shopping or out on a date. When things went wrong I would crash into a severe depression.

In the old days they called it "manic depression". I was not taking any medication but I had the support of my parents to help me through bad times. I had not been seeing a therapist since my teen years. I did not have coping skills.

I dated on and off but the men I chose were usually alcoholics. I did not care much about sex but I liked to go out dancing and to a movie.

I spent a lot of time with my best friend from fifth grade. She was like a sister to me. We went shopping, to the movies, and hung out at her pool in the summer.

In 1983, I left the engineering firm to attend college at a local college in Wollaston, a suburb of Quincy. I felt bittersweet about leaving my job but I needed a change. My supervisor told me I was making a mistake by leaving my secure job. I wanted to go to college. I only had two more years on my father's G.I. Bill. I wanted to prove my guidance counselor wrong. She said I would never be anything except a "teacher aide".

When I first started college I loved my classes and professors. I had a quest for learning and I studied hard. I wanted to be a child psychologist but I did not have the time. I switched my major to Early Childhood Education with a minor in psychology. I was disappointed but I had no other choice.

Despite my pleasure of being a college student, depression started to creep back into my life with a vengeance. I was getting angry again too. I never understood my behavior and why it was so strange. I only knew I could not control it.

In my second year of college I became ill. I lost a great deal of weight and developed a rash. I had attributed this ailment to stress staying up late at night to study for finals, worrying about school and grades.

My mother insisted that I go to a doctor. My father drove me to a local Boston Hospital. The endocrinologist diagnosed me with having a non-malignant tumor on my adrenal gland. She said that was the cause for my mood swings and depression. She put me on medication and I felt better. I gained weight and the rash cleared up. I continued on with school.

I was doing well until I had to take piano lessons and failed them. In my student teaching program I had a conflict with the teacher who taught the preschoolers in Kinder Haus. I almost had a nervous breakdown that time. I hated to go to the Kinder Haus on my scheduled days. I stayed up all hours of the night to try to make my lessons plans perfect. My mother went to talk to Mrs. Carson, who was the supervisor of the program. She told her I was under tremendous stress but I wanted to complete my course and graduate. I did graduate from college on May 26, 1986 with an Associate Degree in Liberal Arts. I was exhausted but felt a surge of relief.

Chapter Four

Trying to Survive in the World Hindered by Mental Illness

After graduation I had a string of jobs at day cares that did not work out and did not pay ANYTHING. I regretted leaving my job as mail clerk but it was too late. Everyone said I should have taken elementary education instead. The Associate Degree was hard enough for me to obtain. I began to feel very depressed about my future. My personal life was shot to hell. The man I wanted to marry did not want to leave his parents and my father had prostate cancer. My mother was suffering from depression too.

My life got much worse. In 1989 I lost my job at a day care center I really enjoyed. My father was dying and I broke up with my boyfriend. I was at a really dark low place in my journey. I started to experience panic attacks. I did not know at the time what was happening to me. I went to church or the grocery store and I was frozen in fear. My heart would pound, I could not breathe, I felt like I was going to faint. I thought I was dying. I did not want to leave he house any more. I used to go to bed with a book and read until I fell asleep. Sleep was my only escape that brought me peace.

My parents were at their wits end. I went to a doctor who diagnosed me with panic disorder. He prescribed Xanax for me, which helped relieve my anxiety.

My father died of liver cancer on May 20, 1990. My world felt like it had collapsed. I was left with my mother. She was strong willed but also a whiner. After the funeral I did my best to tend to her needs and help her around the house. She did not drive so I took her wherever she needed to go. Her health began to fail and she went to the hospital a lot. We fought about how I felt used and how I was doing "all the dirty work," as I called it. Pierre and Jo Ann, my brother and sister never helped. They lived their lives as they pleased.

I sunk into a major depression. I could not get a job for almost a year because of the failing economy. I did have a few temporary jobs but I needed steady work. In 1994, they build a super Stop and Shop in my town. I applied for a service clerk position and was hired I also did food demos for a local company.

I had always wanted a dog and convinced my mother to let me have one of my sister's puppies from one of her litters. He was a cute mixed breed that I named Justin. I loved him dearly. He had behavior problems and my mother wanted to give him away. I was heartbroken and furious with her for making me give him up. She said I could have a small dog so we purchased a chocolate brown mini poodle. I named him Jon Pierre. He was the love of my life and I doted on him. Some days were good but some days were unbearable.

My mother and I were at war again yet I felt I needed her and could not bear life without her.

Chapter Five

Could the Cycle of My Life
Get Any Worse?

I had many episodes where I shopped excessively and I thought that material things would make me happy. I became obsessed with animals taking a vet technician course and adopting animals over the Internet.

I had issues with anger. I was angry at my brother and I wrote him nasty letters. I told him what I thought of him and his wife. I did not stop to think that my impulsive behavior would come back to bite me in the butt. I destroyed my future. He saved all the letters.

I was working three part time jobs in 2003. I worked in two daycare centers and Trudy's as a service clerk three nights a week. My life was about to get very scary for a spell.

I lost my puppy mill rescue dog Lucy to high blood sugar. I lost both my day care jobs due to unfortunate circumstances. My mother had broken her hip and suffered a mild stroke. She had to have surgery and go to rehab to learn to walk again. I tried to take care of the house, dogs, and two birds. My mother came home and for a while everything seemed FINE. I got a job as a substitute teacher and continued my three-hour shifts at Trudy's. I had rescued two new dogs. I felt like everything was going to be all right. It was too good to be true.

One day in the summer of 2005 Pierre came to the house with the box of letters I had written. He talked to my mother in the yard. When she came in the house she was crying. Pierre had left and I asked her, "What was wrong?" "I'm so afraid Pierre is going to put me out of the house?"

I asked her, "Why, what has he done?" She would not tell me. I had this scary odd feeling that something terrible was going to happen. I went to the park in my town, parked the car and sat down on the bench. Deep in my heart I knew it was over. I knew that Pierre and Dawn were going to put us out of our home and that is what they did.

In 2004, I had a boyfriend that had come back into my life. We had a on and off relationship since I was 19 years old. I only liked him as a friend and did not want to marry him. My mother, on the other hand wanted me to date him again. When I protested she said, "Someday you will need him. Be nice to him." I was not thrilled with dating Robert again because of his strange behavior and his drinking, but I did go out with him. In March of 2005 I was still very sheltered, restless and bored. All that was about to change.

Chapter Six

Going From a Nice Home Living in the Suburbs to Being Homeless

I had a week off from work and I thought it would be nice to treat my mother for lunch one day. We lived in a nice quiet suburb so the drive to the restaurant was only about thirty minutes away. We had a nice lunch and conversation. I paid the check with my credit card. We were about to leave when the unthinkable happened. My mother used a cane because of her hip. There were a few steps down from the table to the floor. In one quick horrible moment she tumbled off the step and fell onto the cement floor banging her head. I was horrified when she was lying on the floor unresponsive. The staff called 911. They transported her to the local hospital. I followed the ambulance praying she would be all right. I waited alone scared in the waiting room. They finally called me in to see her. She had broken her other hip and needed surgery. The doctors also thought she may have had another stroke. I stayed at the hospital as long as I could but I had to go back to the house to care for the dogs. I had to call my brother to tell him what had happened. His opportunity finally came to put me out of the house.

I went back to the house and Pierre harassed me all week to get out of the house. I had used my own money to purchase oil for the furnace. He kept telling me to get my things and go to Robert's house.

I called Fred, the family lawyer and told him the situation. He told me to, "stay in the house where I had lived all my life and was comfortable."

On March 15, 2006, I had just taken a shower and was ready to go to work when Pierre and Dawn showed up at the house. I called Robert on the phone and he called "911." The Abington Fire Department took me to the hospital. I was so upset. Pierre did not actually assault me at that time because I called the police but I believed HE INTENDED TO.

My dogs were left alone in the house. They took me to a local hospital. The psychiatrist on duty did not believe that my brother tried to harm me. They admitted me. I told the nurse I needed to call my boyfriend to take my dogs out of the house. They wanted the MSPCA to take them. Anna, my niece, told the nurse lies. She said, "I was losing the house and that was why I was upset." I did not lose the house. Pierre forged my mother's name on the deed of the house so he could put his daughter in the house. The staff believed Anna and they wanted the MSPCA to take my dogs.

I screamed, yelled and dropped to the floor. I said I needed to make a phone call. Finally a nurse allowed me to call my neighbor who had the key to my mother's house. I asked her to call Robert so he could take the dogs to his house as soon as possible.

Robert lives in a state of delusion. He did not believe at first that Pierre would harm my dogs. He did go to my mother's house to remove them from the property. He also took the birdcages and the birds. Later, he told me when we went to my mother's house he saw Pierre with a pair of gloves on. He was entering the back room with the sliding door. He did then believe it was Pierre's intent to harm the dogs.

I was transferred to the Hospital in Everett and placed in the psychiatric ward for 3 days. The doctors and social workers wanted to make sure I had a place to go to when I got out. Robert assured them that I did. They released me on March 19, 2006. Thus my descent into hell began.

Chapter Seven

Living at Robert's House Part 1

Robert did take me in when I became homeless but I paid my dues dearly. He owns a little house in a small town but he is a HOARDER. I went from living in a nice home in a beautiful bedroom community to a three-room horror house with no heat. He had two boarders living with him with drug and alcohol problems.

I was determined to get even with Pierre and Fred Marvin, the so-called family lawyer for what they had done to me. Fred helped Pierre forged my mother's name on the deed of her house. He purchased the house for one dollar. At this time, Pierre and Dawn owned a local bed and breakfast at the Cape in Massachusetts. They no longer own and operate the Inn. They convinced my mother to sign a second deed giving them the right to my childhood home. I had hired a handwriting expert to prove that Pierre committed forgery. I never saw my mother after March 11, 2006. She passed away and they never notified me. I came across her obituary on my YouTube page. They did this deliberately.

The night I got to Robert's house I only had a few clothes to wear because Pierre changed the locks in my mother's house so I could not get my things. Later I was able to get some of my things for a few hours. He hired a policeman to watch the house. He kept my bed, clothes, and some of my belongings.

It was freezing in Robert's house and I did not have a private place to sleep. I was forced to sleep in his cluttered, unkempt bedroom. I had to give up my job at the health care center taking care of children because Pierre kept the car and Robert had to work during the mornings. I had to keep my job at Trudy's because I was not on social security disability yet and that was my only source of income.

Upon my arrival I wrote out a check for heat to be put into the aging furnace I needed to go to work on Sunday. Robert went off with his drunkard friends and had no intention of taking me to work. I was panicking and I decided that I was going to walk the streets of the town I resided in to Abington to get to work. I was upset. When the hospital released me they gave me a number to call the crisis center and I called them. They called the local police and they picked me up and brought me back to the house. I called Robert and I did get to work. Every day that I had to get to work was a struggle. I had to beg, borrow and steal to get there. I gave him money constantly and he still did not want to take me. He was always late picking me up or he did not show up because he was drinking in a bar room.

I took taxis when I could and one time he made me walk from one town to four towns in ninety-degree weather. I began to hate him for all of these events.

Back tracking a bit a few years earlier, I did not have any family or friends to turn to so I turned to Tom. He was a dirty old man that I met at Stop & Shop several years ago. I moved into his house with him for about two weeks in 2007 while Robert bought a trailer from his sister for John to live in.

I had lost everything. My mother, my home, my jobs and my clothes. My life was a mess. I hated my mother for not leaving me the house; I hated my brother and his wife for putting me out. I hated Fred for playing the biggest role in this scenario.

In my frustration and fury I began to write letters to Pierre again. I told him I was going to get even with him for what he had done to me. I accused him of raping me when I was fifteen (he did not). I wrote letters to Fred and made inappropriate phone calls. I know this behavior was not RIGHT. I felt justified at the time because of the treatment I received from Pierre, Dawn and Fred. They did not care about me. They just cared about the money and Anna's welfare.

I take full responsibility for my actions today. I have paid a HUGE PRICE for my MISTAKES. If I had a second chance now and I was in that position I would have handled the situation differently. I am more mature and have learned how to use my wise and rational mind. I have been working on myself everyday to be a better person. I am a work in progress.

In the summer of 2006 Robert was out with his friends. I needed to get out of the house for a while so I went to the local Friendly's for an ice cream. I walked back to the house and when I got there the local police arrived. They approached me. It never occurred to me that they were there to arrest me. I asked them if "something had happened to Robert." "No," they said, "we're here to arrest you for harassing your sister in law." They slapped handcuffs on me. I yelled to John to call Robert so he could look after the dogs. They took me to the police station, fingerprinted me, looked through my purse, and took my belongings. They locked me in the cell. I was scared. It was the first time I had ever been in jail in my life. They allowed me a phone call and I called my friend Tom to come bail me out.

The bailiff said I only had so much time to spare. Robert was called and I was bailed out of jail. I had to go to court and I needed a lawyer. Tom took me to Barnstable where I hired Fritz Martin to defend me.

Another descent into hell again. I had to appear in court many times and I was put on probation. I could never get to the Cape to meet with my probation officer. I never committed any crimes. I just wrote letters saying that Pierre and Dawn were "jerks." They lived in California and NEVER HELPED with my mother. TRUE FACTS!

In June 2007 I tried to renew my driver's license at the Department of Motor Vehicles. When it was my turn to go up to the window they said someone stole my identity. I went to the police department. I explained the situation to the officer on duty. He told Robert and I to sit and wait. He came back in a few minutes and said he had, "good news and bad news." The good news was that no one had stolen my identity. The "bad news" was there was a warrant for my arrest. I was going to jail again. They went through the same procedure as the time before. The bailiff told me I could sit there all night. I did not answer him but my heart sank. In a moment's notice hs said, "You know what? I am going to give you a break, but you have to promise to go to court tomorrow or you will be back in jail." I promised him I would.

The court was in Orleans, but Robert took me to court. I went through a long process to get my name cleared. I had to promise the judge I would never write Pierre and Dawn letters again. It cost me one hundred dollars to get my license back. I never did write a letter to them again. You would think that the universe would have given me a break. I had been to hell and back the last two years. There was more misery to come. I would not have enough notebooks to write about all the terrible things that happened to me.

In 2008, I almost had a cardiac arrest from an allergic relation to medication I was taking for a very bad sinus infection. When I was in the ambulance I heard the paramedics say they thought they were coming in with a "cardiac arrest". I felt myself slipping away. I had hoped to leave this life because of all the pain I have endured. However my Higher Power had different plans for me. I survived that cold winter night in February. I still had a lot of more pain and disappointment to go through. I have to believe my High Power has a purpose for me to be on this planet.

A friend of mine says that, "I get all the shit in life." It scares me to think she is right. I take one step forward and ten back. I have no control over people, places or things. I believe in the serenity Prayer. I ask my Higher Power to take care of me, make the next day better, and give me strength to carry on.

Chapter Eight

Living at Robert's House Part 2;
More Losses and Setbacks

Well the story continues. I wanted to buy a car so I would not have to walk everywhere. I asked Robert to help me find one. BIG MISTAKE! He found me a black Ford that I paid $2,500 for. He said I was not going to get anything better for that price. The car was a lemon from day one. I put him on my insurance as a second driver because I had panic attacks and could not drive to work He drove me to work but he constantly complained about the car. He said it was not safe and the windows did not defrost. I tried to keep up with the repairs and inspection stickers. I only drove the car to the gym and took the dogs for rides locally. Robert drove it most of the time.

On a lighter note, in the summer of 2008 I was searching for a Teacup Yorkie on the Internet. I found a beautiful little female that I had to have. Her name was Susie Q. She was expensive but I felt I deserved her. I contacted the breeder and told her I wanted her. Robert drove me to the bank. I sent Nan Neeman a cashier's check and made arrangements for Susie Q to be picked up at the airport.

I had to work that night so Robert went to pick her up and brought her to work. I was in love immediately she was so beautiful. I held her in my arms and knew there was a God. Maybe things were going to turn around for me. God knew I had plenty of pain in my life, losing everything, spending time in hospitals, shelters and renting a horrible room. I went home feeling elated. I adored Susie Q and my other dogs liked her too. My happiness only lasted for about five minutes. The door in Robert's house did not work. You could not open or close it with a key.

I begged for him to fix the door but he just ignored it. It was August 5, 2008. The worst day of my life! Susie Q was gone forever, why? I had paid my dues that year. Robert drank and the house was a mess. I wished I had died in the ambulance that cold winter night.

To make matters worse I had a so-called friend named Frank Olan. To me he was only a friend but he wanted more. I believed he stole my dog and gave her to the dog officer to get even with me. I would not have sex with him.

As I sit here and write these accounts it is terribly hard and painful to relive all of it. I went with my friend Pam on August 5 to have a cup of coffee at Honey Dew. I had a gate and indoor pen for Susie Q. I left her behind the gate in her purple hair ribbon. She had just been groomed. I told her I loved her and I left the house. I kick myself everyday for not putting her in her pen. When I came back to the house the dog was gone.

I could not open the door because whoever let her out jammed the chair against the door. I called the fire department. They came, opened the door and left. When I entered the house Susie Q was gone. I yelled and screamed and literally peed my pants. I called 911 and Robert came back to the house. I was hysterical!

The police and the dog officer came but they had no interest in Susie Q. They were more concerned about the stray cats in the neighborhood. The dog officer called the MSPCA on me to report me for animal neglect because she thought the stray cats were mine. I was so mad at Robert for not fixing the door. I had to take the cat to the vet and pay $112.00. she had an eye infection but she was not even mine. I told Robert to take me to the hospital. I hated him so much for all the pain he caused me. I really wanted to kill him. He took me to the Hospital where they admitted me to the Psych ward for seven days.

Robert promised to look for Susie Q. He did make up flyers and put them around town. I wanted to curl up in a ball and die. Something inside me knew I would never see her again. I tried to fight the madness. I went to groups, talked to doctors and social workers. I could not stop crying. I made phone calls to animal hospitals, shelters, the MSPCA, to no avail. The doctors and social workers asked Robert to come to the hospital. They asked him if I should go back to his house.

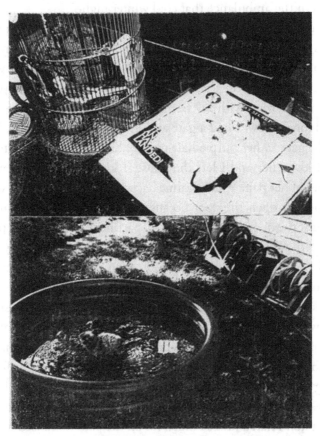

Top photo is a cockatiel named Michael
Bottom photo was my dog, Fatima

He did not know what to say. He said he know I would be okay even if I never got Susie Q back. I was so numb but I knew I had to get back to my other dogs and work. I confirmed what he said. I would never be the same. I thought I would never forgive him. I despised him. I am still upset today about what happened to Susie Q but I forgive Robert to set myself free.

I was sick with worry. I did not know where Susie was. Was she scared? Was someone hurting her? Did she miss me? Was she cold, hungry, lonely? Unfortunately, life went on. However I was obsessed with Susie Q. I was determined to find her. I decided I was going to purchase another Teacup Yorkie. I went back online and found another female. Her name is Fatima. She was a little Silverback Yorkshire terrier. I love her very much. She will never take the place of Susie but she had been a lifesaver for me.

When I lost Susie I prayed all the time. I tried to bargain with God. I told him I would do whatever he wanted as long as I got Susie back. I was irrational and delusional. I felt alone and miserable. No one understood how much pain I was in. Surely Robert did not. When he left for work in the morning I would care for my pets, go back to bed feeling depressed, empty, and wishing I were dead.

One morning I got up and grabbed a phone book. I searched for a private investigator. I called and asked him to find my dog. I paid him too much money and he could not locate her. I was furious at Robert I lost Susie Q and my life savings. I blamed him all the time calling him every name in the book. He had a friend that was a PI. He was a former police officer. He was a real bad apple. I was desperate. He never found Susie. I was devastated. I lost my faith and hope.

I found solace in my other dogs and Fatima. Yet I missed Susie terribly.

The word was out that the dog officer in town sold Susie Q. She called me one day and asked me for her paper work. She said that was the only way I could get my dog back. I made copies of her paperwork and dropped them off at the police department. I was very vulnerable and naïve. I thought that maybe she was the one last person who would help me to get Susie back. She sold my dog. She lost her job, but not for selling Susie. She tried to sell someone else's dog and got caught. The women got her dog back.

Losing Susie Q left me in a delicate state of mind. God could not be so cruel. He would give her back to me. He never did! I spent thousands of dollars on investigators, and advertisements and she was gone forever. There were a lot of false alarms but there was no action. I can only hope that she is in a loving, caring home. I know she does not remember me but I will never forget her. I will never stop loving her it. It is a double-edged sword! Bittersweet. I hate her too for all the pain and anxiety she caused me from losing her. I know it was not her fault, she is only a dog. She did not ask to be stolen.

I made hundreds of novenas, prayed, cried, and walked the streets screaming my head off. I will never understand why God took her from me.

Losing Susie Q left me in a thick haze. I was not thinking clearly. I became obsessed with Teacup Yorkies and proceeded to purchase a small two-pound "Hot Pocket" who brought me more pain and heartache. You think I would have learned my lesson but I did not. She passed away February 2009 from dental disease. I was once again feeling confused and acting out. I went through motions of going to work, caring for my remaining animals and trying to engage in social activities. I wore the tears of a clown. I tried to laugh on the outside but I was screaming on the inside.

My relationship with Robert was not functional. We fought about money and the condition of the house. He did not want to take me anywhere. I had my name in housing yet I refused three offers. I had some crazy notion that I was going to get Susie back and that he was going to clean the house and stop drinking. I thought there was going to be a fairy tale ending. None of these things occurred. I had some good days doing things I loved, community theater, singing in choral groups, being an extra in movies. There were very dark days ahead that I knew nothing about. There were days that I felt hopeless, helpless, suicidal and lifeless. I was going to experience some better times but the storm clouds would come back again. Lightening would hit me soon!

Chapter Nine

Brighter Days and Feeling More Hope

The summer of 2010 was the best summer I had at Robert's house. It was not perfect but it was happier than others. I joined the Senior Serenaders at the Senior Center. I love to sing. I was still working at Trudy's a few nights a week. Diane, Pam and I went for a tour at the State House in Boston. We went to Nanstaket Beach. Pam and I went to Lowell to see the sights and take a boat ride. We went to see Dr. Jekyll and Mr. Hyde in Needham. We went to Alex's to see a male Chippendale strip show. Robert, Diane, and I went to a Senior Prom in Dedham. I played Grandma Jo in Willy Wonka and the Chocolate Factory. I guess I had false hope I really thought there was hope for Robert and I to share a mutual relationship.

I was doing new and fun things. He took me to Manchester, New Hampshire to compete in the Kings and Queens Awards Pageant. I sang on the local cable shows. We went to cast parties. I was never as happy as when I *was* living at my mother's house but I believed I had a second chance.

My world was soon to come crashing down and I would fall to pieces again.

Chapter Ten

Another Journey Through the Valley

In 2001, I had to put my oldest poodle Jon Pierre down. He was 17 years old but it broke my heart. The next day September 26th I helped a lady at work to her car with her bundles, she had a small dog in the car, a Shih Tzu. I don't know what possessed me to hug the dog but she bit my nose badly. The lady was upset but said that I should have known better than to put my face in front of a strange dog. I knew she was right. I have dogs too and I would never let someone else do what I just did. The dog bit the inside of my nose and scratched the outside. It hurt a lot but I knew I would survive. I ran to the bathroom to look in the mirror. My nose was bleeding it was a little swollen but it did not look that bad. My boss told me to fill out an accident report. Amanda, a girl that worked at the store drove me to the Hospital. I called Robert and he came to the hospital at 7:00 P.M. the nurse took me into a room in the back of the E.R. at 3:30 A.M. I was still there.

The doctor never came in to treat me. Robert and I got disgusted waiting. He drove to the Good Sam in Brockton. The doctor cleaned my nose with antibiotics wipes and prescribed Augmentin, an antibiotic. I went home and took the medicine with food.

I woke up the next morning with nausea and a terrible case of the runs. Robert took me back to the ER I told the doctor about the side effects of the medication. She told me to stop taking the pills and I did. I tried to go to work but had the runs and on top of that I got a skin irritation on my buttocks. I was in agony. I could barely walk and I had to pull in carriages.

I was worried that I was going to have a scar on my nose. I bought the scar zone and vitamin E cream. The scar did fade. I had learned later that I had a bout with something called C. diff.

I was pretty miserable from September to the end of November. I filed a Workman's Compensation form but never received any benefits. I had to pay for all the medication and the diaper rash cream out of my pocket.

I was beginning to feel like Job again. Still I tried to carry on with all my responsibilities. In March, I had the pleasure of competing in my third Kings and Queens Pageant. I won trophies, prizes, and the talent contest. 2011 had come to an end. I was heading into a new year. I did not know I was going to ride the year like a roller coaster ups and downs! There were more downs than ups.

Let me take some time to go back to the winter of 2010. Robert needed to have surgery in January. He had a rare birth defect that caused his fingers to curl under. He was having trouble picking things up. On a cold Monday morning in January we went to a hospital in Quincy. He was scheduled for day surgery. They took him to the operating rom. I waited in the lounge for hours. No one came to tell me how he was doing or even acknowledge that I was there. Finally I went to the desk and asked the nurse how Robert Maming was doing. She made a few calls and said he would be out of the recovery room soon.

He came out with his right hand bandaged and in a sling. I had to drive him home. When he got home he changed his clothes and went to bed.

He was out of work six months. I thought I would go out of my mind. I paid for everything, the oil in the furnace, the electric bill and the phone. I gave him money for gas.

I was feeling resentful but at the same time I realized that he gave my animals and I a roof over our heads. Back to the saga of his fingers. He had to go to occupational therapy and in the process they pushed him too hard too soon. He wound up having an infection and spending three days in the hospital on antibiotics. I was scheduled to work on one of the nights he was in the hospital. I was grateful that my friend Diane drove me to work and picked me up to take me home.

In 2011, I had been going to day treatment at Cherry Street in Brockton three days a week. I saw my psychiatrist, Dr. Graham, once a month for obtaining medications. I was singing in the summer shows with the Dedham chorus. I went to practice on Fridays with a friend of mine. Good days, bad days, most of them bad. Robert had a car that had a radiator problem. He had stop to put water in it every few miles. We always ended up fighting whenever we went somewhere.

In the spring, I saw an audition for a show with an acting group in Duxbury called The Man Who Came to Dinner. He did take me to many auditions and rehearsals even though I paid for the gas and I got the third degree from him. We went to Legion Hall in Duxbury. I auditioned for the part. A few days later the director called me. He told me I got a part as a radio announcer. It was a small part but I took it. I did the show and we went to some very nice cast parties.

That summer we also went to see Godspell in Duxbury. The play was put on by a Christian performing group and was in a church. The show was great. They had a nice reception afterward. Everything was fine until I went home and ended up falling when I went to get something out of my organizer. I went to the ER because I injured my knee. More fighting crept into 2012 too.

I did another Kings and Queens's pageant in 2012. 2012 was bittersweet. The fall came, the same routine. He worked at the cemetery. I still worked at the public school as a substitute teacher aide. I found a therapist close to the house and her name was Betty Rowe. Mass Health took care of part of the plan for treatment. I had to pay a co-payment of $20.00 weather permitting I would walk to her office or take a taxi. In the beginning I felt that she was helping me. She even came to one of my performances. Other times it felt she and I did not connect. I had been through a number of therapists. Some came to the house and lasted a few weeks. Others I went to their offices to see.

My problems with Robert were insurmountable. There was no therapist that could work magic in my life. I had suicidal thoughts all the time, to make a long story short. She did try to find me a place to live and people to adopt my dogs. I declined on both offers. I was not ready to leave Robert's house.

Selena

Chapter Eleven

Job Had Nothing on Me

I had auditioned for a chorus part in a fundraiser. It was January 2013. I was in rehearsal in Hingham. I got on the stage to sing a number with the chorus. I was recovering from a cold but all of the sudden I could not breathe. I was wheezing and I was scared to death. I came down from the stage and went to the table where my belongings were. I was crying.

The director of the Cabaret started yelling that we needed to get back on stage to rehearse. There were a couple of nurses in the cast. I told someone that I was sick and could not go back on stage to rehearse. One of the nurses asked me if I had asthma. I said, "no." I did not know why I could not breathe. She told me I was pale and asked if I wanted them to call 911. I said, "no," again. I called Robert and told him to come get me. In the meantime, they opened the armory door and put a chair near the door. I sat in the freezing cold trying to gulp air into my lungs. They tried to distract me by talking to me, I was petrified. I had never experienced such difficulty breathing. I thought I was going to die. Robert finally came to drive me to a hospital on the South Shore. When I arrived there they took my vital signs in the triage. They put me in a bed in one of the ER rooms. The doctor listened to my lungs and ordered a nebulizer treatment.

They diagnosed me with chronic bronchitis and sent me home. This was another descent into the fires of hell with my health. I tried to go back to the cabaret but on the opening night of the show I had a severe panic attack. The ambulance came to the armory to assess my situation. They said my oxygen level was good but that I should not proceed with the show.

Robert drove me to the Hospital again. I sent him home to take care of the dogs. I told him I would call when the doctor knew what the outcome would be. They put me on a heart monitor. I waited scared, anxious and alone. The doctor came to see me and said they were going to admit me to the hospital. I would stay in the ER that night and in the morning I would go to the cardiac care unit. I called Robert. He said he would come in the morning. They thought there was a problem with my heart. I flipped out on the inside. This really put the cherry on the cake. The next day was Saturday. I had bought Robert a ticket for the show. I wanted him to attend. I had worn one of my mother's blouses as part of my costume and left it at the armory. I wanted him to retrieve it for me. It had sentimental value. I never got it back.

I spent the weekend attached to the heart monitor. I was scheduled for a CAT scan and a stress test. The doctors told me that my lungs were compromised but they never confirmed that I had asthma. My roommate was an older lady who had asthma but she was being treated for congestive heart failure. Naturally they would focus on her more than me.

On Sunday I went for the stress test on the treadmill. I thought I would surely have a heart attack. The doctor put the treadmill on fast speed. He told me there was "nothing wrong with my chest." They sent me back to my room. Robert was there waiting for me. I was still having trouble breathing. My doctor came into the room and said my heart was fine. She sent me home with inhalers. I went home with a heavy heart knowing this ordeal was not over.

I continued to get worse and I went to many doctors getting different diagnoses. I knew I was experiencing high anxiety as well.

I remember one night in 2013, when I went to a local Brockton hospital when I was having trouble breathing. The doctor ordered a chest x-ray. He was looking at the pictures and I was sitting in my bed watching TV I had this feeling like a "black cloud" was hanging over my head. Robert was with me. I heard the doctors say that I had "emphysema or bad asthma". He came back to my room and was very nasty. I don't remember his name but I do remember that he had no "beside manner." He was tall, dark and handsome. He handed me a card with the name of a specialist in lung disorders and told me to contact him. I was frightened and I carried on. He told me point blank to stop coming to the E.R. he said there were "sick people," he needed to take care of whose oxygen level was 79% or 80%. I was livid! I left the hospital that night in a bad state of mind. I was angry at God! I was angry at life in general. My mind went to a very dark place.

I blamed Robert for not cleaning the house or taking care of me, and I blamed my mother for suggesting he was right for me. I began to write letters again. I did not even care if I got into trouble with the law. I wrote a letter to a girl I know. We will call her "Jane" (which is not her real name). I knew her from an event that we both were in. I had lost an item and she said she would try to help me find it. She never did. I had written a terrible letter to the facility where the event took place. I swore at her and called her unacceptable names.

I called the facility crying once it dawned on me how damaging the letter would have been to me. The lady that answered the phone was truly an "angel". I explained the situation to her and told her I was truly sorry for writing this letter to "Jane". She destroyed the letter and thank God "Jane" never found out. We still speak today.

I had written a letter to the doctor that treated me, which he did receive. I continued to go to doctors who told me I had COPD, chronic bronchitis and emphysema, which would never be reversed. I refused to accept the diagnosis.

I had gone to my mother's primary care physician for years but I was unhappy with the care he had given me. I had a bad case of bronchitis at the time. The doctor's office was about an hour and a half from where I lived. I was late getting there and very upset. I could not breathe. The nurses were impatient with me. I wanted to find another doctor so I did a search on the Internet. I had been on Prednisone for my lungs. The drug has a lot of side effects, depression and suicidal thoughts. I was going through a difficult time. Robert's house was not clean and the furnace was not safe.

I do believe that the furnace played a role in my lung disease. One of the doctors I had seen said my lungs were oblong. They looked like lungs of a smoker. I had never smoked in my life. On one of my appointments to see Dr. Carl Mooney, my allergy doctor, he ordered a nebulizer. I was very nervous at first taking these treatments. The albuterol that is inhaled into the lungs with the aid of this machine causes anxiety.

Robert lives in the house with the dust, dirt, and allergens but he does not have asthma. The visiting nurses who showed me how to operate the nebulizer said the house needed more ventilation. I was beside myself with anger and depression. I was in a deep dark hole.

I had chances to get into housing before all this happened but I sabotaged every opportunity. I was afraid to make a move even though his house was completely unlivable. I was feeling sorry for myself. I had a classic case of "why me?" I served God all my life and was devoted to Jesus. Now he abandoned me in my urgent need. I began to call emergency services such as the Board of Health, Emergency Housing Resources, and the Department of Housing. All of these agencies could not help me. The head of the Board of Health in the town said she only handled health issues in commercial situations. She did not handle residential issues.

I was desperate and impulsive. I needed to get out of Robert's house as soon as possible before I died of an asthma attack. I was afraid I was going to stop breathing. I was having a nervous breakdown. I had stopped taking the Prednisone Dr. Turney told me it was causing a problem. For my depression and panic. He told me I had a mild case of "asthma" but in my mind I believed that my lungs were in terrible shape. I thought I as going to stop breathing at any moment. I went to the hospital and was admitted to the psych ward for eleven days with major depression and anxiety.

On a lighter note, I had times in the nine years that were brighter. I always had hardships since I became "homeless" in 2006 but I did have enjoyable moments. This story is about my dark journey with depression and anxiety. I have had very sad, difficult times in my life. Suffering is a part of life for everyone, rich, poor, smart, handicapped, black and white, beautiful, old, or young.

Some people seem to suffer more than others. Everyone suffers to some degree. If we are alive we will suffer. I have suffered both mentally and physically and I find that the mental aspect is much worse. I choose to believe in a Higher Power but that does not make me exempt from the suffering in this world. On the contrary there are many obstacles in my path that I must try to overcome. I have to make a choice each day to choose whether I will be content or miserable in my circumstances. I choose to be happy.

Chapter Twelve

Learning to Use Coping Skills and Accepting What I Cannot Change

In 2012, I had struggles and triumphs. I published a fiction story called Diana's Story which I am proud of. I had many allergy tests that proved I am not allergic to any foods. I do not have a chronic obstructive pulmonary disease (COPD). I do have asthma but it is under control. I struggled with depression, anxiety and worry about my finances. Robert and I did not see eye to eye on anything. I lost my job at Trudy's due to health reasons and a lack of transportation. I have an apartment that I moved into. I continued to participate in shows and plays. There were darks and bright days. My four dogs brought me a source of comfort but they were a lot of work and worry.

I spent time in hospitals and respites in Norwood and Milford. I felt hopeless and thought about ending my life. Christmas I got the flu and it messed up my asthma. I was in the hospital New Years Eve and Day at a local hospital in Brockton.

In January I had another breakdown and was hospitalized.

Robert lost his job at the cemetery and his car was repossessed. He could not get to work as a security guard. The tension between us was thick. I had to take taxis to get to my apartment and the bank. I now have an account with the Ride and I have good friends who help me. My life is not perfect nor will it ever be. I AM A SURVIVOR.

I am trained to be a presenter for NAMI. In our own voice presentations sponsored by the National Alliance of Mental Health. I like telling my story to people who have a mental illness to give them hope. Faith makes things possible but never easy.

Now 2012 and 2013 were not a picnic in the park but I got through the storms of my life. I was glad to see 2012 go by and try to make a fresh start in 2013. 2013 I was in for a roller coaster ride. My Christmas was not that great. I took a taxi to my apartment and when the taxi dropped me off someone stole my food bag. I left the bag just for a second at the door of my building. I use the stairs instead of the elevator. I carried my other bags up first. I went back to retrieve my bag. It was gone. I could not believe it. I called the police and they made a report and came to my apartment with emergency food. There was nothing else they could do. The only good thing was that I transferred my tablet and gift certificate to my other bag. That Christmas "sucked" to say the least.

I was alone without friends and family. 2014 was next on the agenda. I did not know what I was in for. January through February had ups and downs in the weather as well as my life. I worked some times as a substitute teacher aide in the school system. I was licensed to work in a local day care as a regular assistant.

It was a nightmare to obtain that piece of paper. I had to take online classes the summer before. I had the problem of my C.O.R.I. The department of criminal justice did not want to submit the certificate to me. I wrote to the Orleans Court to have my record sealed and they gave me a date in December of 2013. Robert and I had to take a 6:00 AM train to South Station and get a bus to Orleans's Court. The weather was raining and snowing. We had a 2:00 PM appointment. The judge allowed me to seal my record and we left. We caught a bus back to South Station. We got home at 11:30 that night.

Back to the year 2014, I was still working. Robert and I were feuding over money, the unclean conditions of the house and his lack of concern for important matters. I had anger and resentment toward him. I always felt like I was on the edge even though I saw a psychiatrist and a therapist. I had suicidal thoughts. I was restless and anxious. I was also frozen with fear.

I put $300.00 worth of oil in the burner but when he turned it on the heat did not come on. Smoke and fumes came pouring out of the oil tank. I was furious. I had difficulty breathing and the fumes were overwhelming.

He went into the basement to seep up the oil that spilled onto the floor. He opened the door for ventilation. I called the Fire Department. They came to assess the situation. They said there was not any carbon monoxide but not to turn on the oil burner. Robert and I were enemies on the battlefield again. I told him I wanted him to pay me back the money I spent buying oil. I did not think he would follow through with his promise. He was so accustomed to lying. It is normal for him to tell one lie after another. He did sell some of his mother's jewelry and paid me some of the money. It was freezing and we were left with one electric heater. We went to Rite Aid and I bought the display for $100.00. I thank God that I did because the temperature dropped to nine degrees, 17 and the 20's. We had heat in the house but there was no heat in our relationship. We were as cold as ice.

I was volunteering at a fitness center in child care. I had a gym membership that I never used. I walked the track a few times before my shift. I used the showers when Robert had to turn off the hot water. I stopping paying the electric bill because he never cleaned the house. I had paid $700.00 electric bills for years but when I got my apartment I could not do it anymore. One year the electric company attached the bill to my apartment and I had a hell of a time trying to straighten it out.

The struggles still continued through March and April. When Robert had money he would go to the bar room and drink. Sometimes I would follow him down there and rant and rave at him to come home. Sometimes he would, sometimes he would not.

April 15, 2014, was a very rude eye opener for me. We had a disagreement and he went to the bar room. I should have never said that damaging phrase, "Don't bother to come home." He left the house at 7:00 PM. I fell asleep on my bed. He came through the door at 12:30 AM. He was very intoxicated and angry. He woke me up out of a sound sleep and announced that he was going to, "kill me" and "my therapist." I felt instant fear and a sense of alarm. I knew this time was different. He was volatile. When he is intoxicated he rants and raves. He is extremely obnoxious. He went into the kitchen to make himself a sandwich but I felt terribly unsafe. I knew he had guns in the house and ammunition. I feared he may harm me and my Teacup Yorkie Fatima. I ran outside. It was 1:00 AM. I dialed 911 and told the dispatcher the situation.

They sent police cruisers down to the top of the street. They asked me if I were injured. I said, "no", but I was very afraid that he would do something violent. They did not know about the guns but I felt that I had to tell them. They asked me if I could identify the type of guns he owned. At that moment, I could not think straight enough to remember if they were handguns or rifles. It turns out they were rifles. They told me to stay where I was and wait for them to return. I mumbled that he was alcoholic and needed rehabilitation.

In my numb mind I thought they would arrest him and take him to detox they came back to get me about 45 minutes later. I saw him on the ground handcuffed. He asked them, "What did I do?" They led me into the house and said, they had to take him to the hospital because he was injured. They also said he was "violent" and it was not safe for me to be in the house. They said he would be in the hospital for a few days and then he would be released. They asked me where the guns were. I had no choice but to tell them. They retrieved the guns and the ammunition. It was a horrible night. When they left I could not sleep. I was depressed, scared and angry. I wondered where God was throughout this mess. I cleaned the birdcages, took my nebulizer treatment and swept the floor. I laid down at 6:00 Am. I woke up at 8:00 and felt horrible. I felt like I had been run over by a truck. I was worried about Robert too. Even though he caused me emotional harm I did not want him to die. I called the local Brockton hospital to check on his condition. The nurse asked the doctor if she could give me information. He said, "he guessed so." I was told that Robert had a head injury and was transferred to a prestigious Boston Hospital. The police had used a Taser gun on him because they thought he was armed with a weapon. He fell backwards on his head and suffered a concussion. I called him in the hospital and he was angry and upset. He blamed me for his mishaps. Not the drinking. I was struggling with my own health problems, depression, chronic bronchitis, and a feeling of hopelessness. For the first time since I had known him I was afraid. My friends said I needed to get away form him. My therapist and psychiatrist at the time agreed I should leave the house. I had four dogs, three birds, and a turtle to care for. When he got out of the hospital I asked him if he wanted to attend Alcoholics Anonymous (AA) or therapy. He did not. He was angry with me, my therapist, and the police and the government. He obtained a copy of the police report. I read it and realized how serious the situation was. He could have killed me that night. I came close to death again. I looked at reality. I was very scared but not scared enough to detach from him all the way.

I went to my apartment for a few days to try to unwind. However, I went back to his house again. I can tell you that every time he went out drinking I was filled with fear and anxiety. I kept my coat on, my keys and my cell phone in my hand ready to call 911 when he came in the door. It was a crazy way to live.

In June, more unsuspecting health issues came my way. I had stomach pains that would not go away. I went to the ER and was diagnosed with a bout of colitis. They gave me the CIPRO which gave me the skin rash again.

Chapter Thirteen

Heartbreak and Heartache

The summer was 50/50 for me. Good days and bad. I spent time at my apartment, at the pool, which was nice. I did not work so I had financial problems. I am on Social Security Disability. I have to watch my money. I have to make sure my rent is paid first and then my ride account. I have expenses grooming the dogs and taking them to the vet.

At the end of August, we took my big Yorkie Stevie Nicks to the vet for her annual check-up. They gave her a rabies shot and decided to split up her distemper shot because she had reactions in the past that were bad.

A few weeks later she became ill. She was vomiting and could not keep any food down. I cooked her rice, which seemed to help her for a short time. Soon her symptoms returned. She lost a significant amount of weight. We had transportation problems. We did not get her to a vet in time. I knew she was dying and I left her with Robert. I left a check for him to take her to the vet to be put down. I went to church and prayed to God that if there was no hope for her He would take her to end her suffering. I called Robert Monday morning and he said she was worse. When I returned to his house she had expired. We called his sister and she took us to a local animal hospital in the area. They confirmed her death. I wanted to do an autopsy but Robert said it was too expensive. The cost was five hundred dollars.

I was annoyed, "I thought," who is he to tell me what to do with my money?" Needless to say I never knew why she died. I also had trouble getting her ashes from a pet cemetery in Middleboro, Massachusetts. They misplaced the check I sent them. I sent it certified. I finally did receive her ashes but I was a nervous wreck. Negative things had happened in the fall of 2014. It had taken its toll on me. Many days I felt hopeless and I would go to the hospital.

I had been in the play Oliver with my two friends. I was really having a nice time and looking forward to opening night. The director decided to take away my lines. I was angry and hurt at first and did not want to do the play. I thought about the hard work I had done at rehearsals. I need to be a professional. I did the show and had fun even without my lines. I was not a "quitter" when the going got rough. There were three shows. I also played Aunt Carol in Little Women in Canton Community Theater.

The one bright light had been the NAMI Peer to Peer Training in Boston. I completed the course and received a certificate.

Dark days were coming. I was feeling anger, resentment, frustration and I was lonely. It was almost Thanksgiving. I hated the holidays. I had no family support and I missed Stevie Nicks.

I was taking a shower and Robert came into the house. My heart sank. I knew he was going to drink. He briefly spoke to me and then was out the door. He walked over to Governor's Pub, a local watering hole. It is now Paula's House. I got out of the shower and quickly dressed. I walked to the bar room and tried to get him to come home. He refused. He said it was his "night out." He was sitting there drinking aimlessly. I returned to the house knowing it was going to be another night like April 15. It almost was, but not quite.

It was 7:30 PM. I was furious that he was going to put me through hell again. I prayed to God to keep me safe and give me strength if he came home very intoxicated. Sure enough he did at 1:00 AM. He came into the house very drunk, cursing and swearing. My heart was pounding and I had a tension headache. He went into his bedroom and shut the door. I hoped he would "sleep it off." No such luck! He came out of the room, swearing, slurring his words but saying he was going to kill the police and the government. He fell to the floor kicking my box of clothes off the hope chest. I was terrified. Triggers of the last time came flooding back I called the police again. No need to go through the details. They were the same only this time there were no guns or ammunition. They took him to jail for 12 hours. The Sargent found humor in his crazy behavior. I was not amused. I was disgusted. I was disillusioned as they arrested him. I knew that no matter how hard I tried he was always going to drink. He did not want help. My fear was that some night he was going to get drunk and kill me. He could be violent the police believed he would do harm one day. I am still afraid of him when he is intoxicated.

After he went to jail I knew I had to get away for Thanksgiving. I could not sleep. I repeated my usual routine of cleaning and taking care of the animals. The place was a disaster. I had lost all hope. I fell asleep at 1:00 AM and woke up at 8:00 AM. I was supposed to take an acting class with Pam and Diane that morning. I was exhausted but I knew the class would be good for me. I needed the distraction.

When Pam picked me up I told her what had happened. She was shaken by what I said. She asked me what was I going to do. I told her I would take a taxi to my apartment after the class. She offered to give me a ride after class. Despite everything I really enjoyed the class. I was at the apartment with my Teacup Yorkie Fatima. She really brought me comfort and helped me with my sadness.

The next day was Thanksgiving and I went to a church that hosted a dinner in my town. Pam picked me up at 3:30 to bring me back to Robert's. I had to attend to the other dogs and work at a local church on Sundays. I had dreaded to call Robert to ask if the dogs were all right, but I did. Kelly had looked in on them the day before. My life continues to be a roller coaster ride. Highs and lows in December. High points were singing in choirs and acting in plays. Low points were depression, fighting with Robert, money problems, lack of transportation and Christmas was coming. There would not be any festivities.

Robert's sisters really did not care about our welfare or happiness. Pam and I had a disagreement about three weeks before Christmas. She thought my needs were far greater than she could meet. I was defensive and hurt but I tried to keep a stiff upper lip. I thanked her for her friendship and all that she did for me. (Pam is a beautiful, warm, giving lady who is my best friend and I will always love her!)

I wondered why God had allowed me to go through such pain in my life, over and over again. I felt like dying inside. Why was I always suffering the same cycle of defeat? Why did God hate me? I felt sorry for myself and I felt like a victim of circumstance. I could not do anything about it so I threw in the towel and worked in my shed to stave of my frustration.

When I came back in the house Pam called to apologize. She said she still wanted to be friends and if I needed a ride to the groomer with the dogs to call her. My Higher Power did work out the kinks for me. I just did not trust him enough. Pam came to see me in Little Women and drove me back and forth Saturday.

I got through the play and was hoping to get through December without having to go to the hospital. It was not meant to be. Two weeks before Christmas, Robert and I had an argument on Saturday. It was cold outside and the cold affects my breathing. I walked to the library and by the time I got there I could not breathe. I took a puff of my inhaler and went inside to get my massages from my tablet. I was crying because Robert said he was going to kill me again. The librarian asked me if I was all right. She brought me some water to drink. I called Kelly to ask her for help. She was not at home. I left her a message. I knew I could not walk home and I did not want to take a taxi. The librarian came back and asked me if I was feeling better. I told her I was not. She asked if I would like a policeman to drive me home. I said I would.

The police officer took me back to Robert's house. I knew I needed to go to the hospital. I scraped up enough cash to call a taxi. My cell phone rang. It was Kelley. She drove me to the hospital. They examined me in the ER. I had an asthma attack brought on by the cold and stress. They admitted me for the night. I talked to social workers that suggested I attend women's groups. They gave me a list of shelters to go to in an emergency upon my discharge. I left the hospital feeling dejected.

I had to reschedule the vet appointment for Noelle and Fatima to have their ears rechecked. They both had ear infections.

Cindy, a friend of Robert, drove me to my apartment after the appointment. I was hoping to attend Mass on Christmas day. They say, "We make plans but God displans." I slept well on Monday night. I woke up on Tuesday morning and all "hell broke loose." The minutes on both my cell phones were gone and I did not have a landline phone. I was hysterical. I had given Adam Felos, the owner of (a Brazilian store) more than $100.00. He failed to put minutes on my phone. Man was I screwed! I was screaming at the Assurance Wireless people that I was supposed to have minutes on my phone. I ended up calling 911 and telling the dispatcher I needed help. (You can use the phone for an emergency even if you're out of minutes). I felt very unsafe. I had suicidal thoughts for months. I was admitted to a local Brockton Hospital for eight days with major depression.

Chapter Fourteen

Hope for a Better Year and More

I am now in 2015 and I am going to try to obtain goals. I have to start with small ones. Trying to stay out of the hospital is number one. If I have to go back I won't be too hard on myself. I am not perfect nor will I ever be.

A few weeks I auditioned for a part in a play at a local theater in Norwell. I did not get the part. I was disappointed but I was proud of myself for trying. I will try again in the future. I have to take care of my body and mind. I have to eat right and get enough sleep. I have to remove myself from stressful situations. I have to use coping skills and have an attitude of gratitude, even in little things. I need to forgive others and myself. Forgiveness is a hard issue for me. I am the type of person who always held a grudge. Holding grudges is very unhealthy. Not only for the person who had wronged you but yourself too. Forgiveness sets you free! It does not mean that you have to accept unacceptable behavior but forgiveness helps you move on.

I have goals in 2015. I would like to write a children's book, take a trip, and record a CD of songs I love. These are my dreams. Dreams are important. They give you hope and hope motivates you. I have challenges too. I have to make decisions about my apartment, my animal's treatment and if I choose to rescue more dogs. Robert and I have issues that need to be dealt with in our relationship. It is his choice whether or not he wants to seek help. At any rate, we both have to make a lot of decisions. We have made a lot of mistakes; hurt each other along our journey. We need to make amends. I hope if we can't be a couple, we can remain friends. We have a long history together. Times enmeshed in our hearts and minds.

2015 is just beginning for me. I don't know what joys, sorrows or successes it will bring. I don't know about tomorrow, next week, next year or five years from now. I only have today. Some people's lives are over today. I can only hope they left this earth peacefully, knowing they did what they could do. They had a good journey in their life. I hope that when my time is up I leave this world without bitterness or regrets. Life is too short to hate and be bitter.

I will never be a brain surgeon or a rocket scientist. I will never win a Nobel Peace Prize. I am important to God and myself but I am not better or less than anybody in this ever changing world. I have a purpose and I am loveable and capable. I am deserving of happiness like the whole human race. I should have died a number of times but I did not. I believe my Higher Power has a plan for my life.

It is not to be rich or famous or a super model. I would not mind being any of those things but that is not my destiny. I have suffered many dark days and my journey has been hard. Mental illness is a disease just as asthma and cancer have challenges and pain associated with them. With mental illness you can't see the outward scars but it hurts just the same.

Everyone has problems. Some people go through more than others but no one escapes pain in life. Believe that your Higher Power loves you no matter how many mistakes you have made. I believe that if my story reaches only one person living on the earth I can make a difference in their life. Just as if I were the only person my Higher Power would have died for my sins. Believe your Higher Power will see you through the rest of your life, good times, bad times, in between times and when your life is over he will lead you home.

If you are reading this chapter and thinking about ending your life, don't do it! Most of my life I had suicidal thoughts and attempts but today I know life is precious. It is a gift from God no matter how difficult it may be at times. Problems will come and go. They are temporary. Suicide is permanent! Reach out to someone, anyone who cares about you. There is hope and help out there. There are many resources, National Alliance of Mental Health (NAMI), Samaritans, Crisis Center, hot lines, clergy, therapists. I have provided some information at the back of this book. You can also look on the Internet. If you feel desperate go to your local ER. Just get help.

I included one more chapter in this book about the death of my dog Fatima. My story will never be over. There will be many more changes to take place, but I must end my book now.

I only want to say that I am a "victor", "not a victim".

Thank you for reading this book.

Until we meet again,

Robin S.

Some Resources

- The National Alliance of Mental Illness (NAMI)
    - 1-800-950-6264
- Samaritans – 41 West Street, Boston, MA
    - 617-870-4673
- Brockton Multi Service Center
    - 1-508-897-2000
- Rape Crisis Center
    - 1-508-588-8255

Stevie Nicks , Nicky, and Fatima

Last Chapter

Fatima

I was done with my book but one tragic event had happened that I could not ignore on March 4, 2015. I took my beloved Yorkshire Terrier Fatima to have a dental appointment at the animal hospital in Stoughton. I was advised that she should have one. I was leery about them doing the procedure on her because she was so small. They assured me that they would clean her teeth and only remove BAD TEETH. When I took Fatima to Lila's on Wednesday morning she was a happy, healthy dog. When we went to pick her up at 5:00 PM that was not the case. She was breathing heavy in my friend's car. We were instructed to give her a soft diet, antibiotics and pain killers (they removed 14 of her teeth). She woke up at 12:30 AM Thursday morning and she could not breathe. She was gasping, choking. I freaked out! Robert called his friend and she took us to the emergency Animal Hospital. I had already paid Lila's a thousand dollars. I really could not afford to pay them more money. They did check her out and the vet said she had a minor breathing problem due to an irritation in her throat from the tube they inserted. The problem was that she said to take her back to Lila's because her breathing could become worse. They charged me $114.00. It was 7:00 Am, Robert and I had been up all night. He called his sister and they took us back to Lila's. The vet at Lila's said she was fine. They claimed they did x-rays. We never saw them. They said to take her home and continue to giver her the medication.

The vet at the VCA said her soft vulva tissue was exposed and Dr. Mason at Lila's said he would "push it back in". They charged me another $45.00 for less than a half hour visit. We took her home where she continued to get worse. She could not breathe, eat, walk, or stand. There was nothing I could do for her except hold her, tell her I loved her and I was sorry. She was so scared! The vets at Lila's never gave her anything for her anxiety. I thought she was going to die on my bed. I freaked out again! When Robert came home we took her in a taxi to an emergency center for Animals in Walpole Massachusetts. They immediately put her in an oxygen cubicle. They deemed her the second most critical patient in the unit. We said our goodbyes petting her through the holes on the side of the cubicle.

The next day she threw up bile, coded and died.

We learned that the vet at Lila's, Dr. Kay Blume, who did the procedure on her, collapsed her trachea. She had fluid in her lungs and congestive heart failure. (Note that Lila's Animal Medical Center has never admitted to making any medical mistakes when treating Fatima). My heart is broken. I am devastated. I filed a complaint against Dr. Blume and the hospital. What really hurt me is they knew she was dying but they tried to cover it up. They should have put her to sleep after they botched her surgery. I also believe they were neglectful with my other dog Stevie Nicks after they treated her.

My boyfriend did not want me to take her there in the first place. I wished I never did. These past few weeks have been difficult but they have taught me a lot of lessons in my life's journey. It has been painful. There was no way that I could have known that Fatima would suffer so much and die at the age of seven.

I tried to get justice for Fatima. It did not work. The veterinary board in Boson refuses to hold Lila's accountable for any wrongdoing. My hands are tied.

I loved Fatima very much. I will always remember her but I do not want to remember the images of her dying a slow painful death. I want to remember the happy, cute, barking little girl that she was. She loved to be petted and go for walks in her dog stroller. I have to set her free like a butterfly. I have to set myself free too.

These past two weeks got me thinking about God whom I call my Higher Power. At first I was so angry with him, cursing him and whining. This is the seventh dog I lost in my lifetime. It was not just losing the dog. It was watching the process of death, which is natural. It was just so painful. However, we all have to die sooner or later.

No one likes to talk about death, mental illness, homeless people, or mentally challenged folks. Everyone wants the "perfect people." Beautiful, smart people are always being showcased on television, books, and the media. Phones, watches, and the television are smart these days. I am not against these things but I think being honest, caring and kind is more important than being beautiful.

Fatima's death has changed my attitude and gave me a reality check of what is important in life. I believe my higher power gives people a "free will" and a mind to reason "wrong from right." There will always be tragedy and strife, poverty and sorrow, but we have to live in the moment. We have to be grateful for each and every blessing that comes into our lives. No matter how small. I rescued another little Yorkshire terrier in June of 2015. Her name is Angel. She is pretty, smart and healthy. I think Fatima is smiling from Rainbow Bridge.

Take care of your body and mind, stay calm and carry on.

Robin

Remember there is always hope. If you fall down seven times get up eight, may be not today or tomorrow, but the next day get up! Know that you are someone capable, worthy and deserving to be loved and to love also.

Nicky

Richard Jr.

Fatima,

I am so sorry you had to leave me.

I miss you very much. I miss holding you and petting you. I miss you bending your little blonde head to "give love."

I miss your little paw reaching out for more pets when I stopped petting you.

I miss you turning over for your belly rubs.

The vets that I trusted to care for you betrayed you, me, and all of those who loved you. They were negligent and money hungry. They claim to love animals and want to help sick animals but they lie through their teeth. I will never forget the terror in your eyes as you struggled to breath. I felt so hopeless. All I could do was tell you I was sorry and hold you.

Fatima, you and I have to be bigger than the folks who so cruelly took your life. They tried to cover their tracks. We have to forget them and set ourselves free. Remember the good days. The days we took walks in the park in your dog stroller. The days you swam in your dog pool. The nights we cuddled under the covers. The days you wore your pretty dresses as we walked around town.

Fatima, you brought a lot of love and comfort to me. I will always love you; never doubt that. You are free of the pain and terror of the last days of your life. Run free at Rainbow Bridge with Stevie Nicks, Hot Pocket, Lucy, and Jon Pierre. I am heart broken but do not fret little girl. I will go on. You will always live in my heart and memory. Wait for me Fatima for I hope to return to you soon. I love you.

Your loving mother,

Robin

Index

3. Bronchitis: inflammation of the membranes lining the bronchial tubes.
4. Bedside manner: describes how healthcare professionals handle a patient.
5. Bipolar disorder: chemical imbalance in the brain.

C

1. Cabaret: for entertainment featuring music, songs and dance.
2. Cardiac arrest: and abrupt stop in blood circulating due to a cessation of heart function.
3. Carbon monoxide: indoor carbon, co levels of exposure to poison gas.
4. Chest x-ray: a machine that takes pictures of the chest and lungs.
5. Congestive heart failure: shortness of breath, high blood pressure, endocrine nutritional metabolic immunity disease, ischemic heart disease, diabetes mellitus.
6. Crematory: a furnaces where a corpse cam be burned to ashes.
7. Colitis: inflammatory bowl disease.
8. Cipro: antibiotic for urinary tract infection.

D

1. Depression: a mental state of characterized by a pessimistic sense of inadequacy and a despondent lack of activity.
2. Dr. Golden: a highly trained psychiatrist in Sharon Massachusetts.
3. Delusional: suffering from delusions not in touch with reality.
4. Desperate: hopeless, having little hope of success.
5. Disillusionment: the condition of being disenchanted.

H

1. Hoarder: compulsive hoarding
2. Harassment: a feeling of intense annoyance caused by torment.

I

1. Irrational: not logical or reasonable.

J

1. Job: a biblical figure that suffered for a great many years. He suffered many things and never caused God.
2. Jesus Christ: the Son of God.

M

1. Milton Hospital: Milton, Massachusetts
2. Mental illness: disorder that affects your mood.
3. Manic depression: known as Bi-polar disorder

N

1. Normal: overall typical frequency like "everyone else".
2. Nebulizer: a dispenser that turns liquid such as perfume into a fine mist.

P

1. Psychosis: any severe disorder in which contact with reality is lost or highly distorted.
2. Psychiatrist: a physician who specializes in psychiatry to do with the mind.
3. Panic Attack: periods of intense fear or apprehension of sudden onset accompanied by at least four cognitive symptoms, heart palpitations, dizziness, shortness of breath, irrational fear.
4. Petrified: so frightened that one is unable to move.
5. Prednisone: allergy inflammation autoimmune disease.

R

1. Rehabilitation: program for addicts and people addicted to alcohol and drugs.

S

1. Saga: something that is sad yet comical.
2. Serenity Prayer: God grant me the serenity to accept the things I cannot change, the courage to change the things I can, and the wisdom to know the difference.

T

1. Trucchi's: a grocery store in Abington, Massachusetts
2. Taser Gun: used by police to stun someone who is aggressive.
3. Teacup Yorkie: very small Yorkshire terrier three to four pounds.

V

1. Violent: brutal, vicious, savage.

W

1. Wise mind: place where reasonable mind and emotion despite sometimes uncertain overtake feelings and emotions.

2

1. "2 pack": used to treat lungs infection.

Additional Information

Dedham Chorus
735 Washington Street, Dedham, MA
Director Tammi Allen

Beth Israel Hospital
Boston, MA

Stoughton Senior Serenades
110 Rokland Street
Stoughton, MA 02072
Director: Helyn Hall

Kings and Queens Mini Awards Pageant
Manchester, NH
Director: Bonnie Nettles

Critas Good Samaritan
Norwood, MA

Milton Hospital
South Shore Hospital
55 Fogg Road, Weymouth, MA

Harbor Medical Associates
1690 Main Street, South Weymouth, MA

Dr. John Terzian
771 W. Center Street
West Bridgewater, MA

Hingham Armory
Hingham, MA

Hingham Community Center
70 South Street, Hingham, MA
The Company Theatre
30 Accord Park Drive, Norwell, MA

Stoughton Little Theatre of Stoughton

Avon Community Theatre
Avon Middle High School
Avon, MA

Ramblewoods/Holbrook Apartments
Bay Players, Duxbury, MA
These are fine medical establishments and entertainment sources.

Credits
NAMI National Alliance of Mental Health
The Schrafft Center
524 Main Street Suite 1M17
Boston, MA 02129-1125

The Samaritans
41 West Street #4
Boston, MA 02111

Hospital
Beth Israel Deaconess Medical Center
330 Brookline Ave
Boston, MA

Colleges
Eastern Nazarene College
123 E. Elm Street
Wollaston, MA

Massasoit Community College
One Massasoit Boulevard
Brockton, MA

Printed in the United States
By Bookmasters